The Céline Dion Songbook

Editor: Carol Cuellar

Editor's Note: Warner Bros. Publications Inc.
would like to give special thanks to René Angelil
and Ben Kaye of Feeling Productions, Inc.
for their decision to make Céline Dion
a member of our print family.
We hope Céline will enjoy
her first published songbook.

Management: René Angelil
Feeling Productions, Inc.
4 Place Laval, Suite 500
Laval, Quebec
Canada H7N 5Y3
Management Contact: Mr. Ben Kaye

Book Design: Odalis Soto

(From Walt Disney's "BEAUTY AND THE BEAST")

Beauty And The Beast

Lyrics by
HOWARD ASHMAN

Music by
ALAN MENKEN

Female: Tale as old as ____ time, *Male:* song as old as ____ rhyme. *Both:* Beau-ty and the ____

Beast.

Beau-ty and the Beast. _____

Only One Road

Words and Music by
PETER ZIZZO

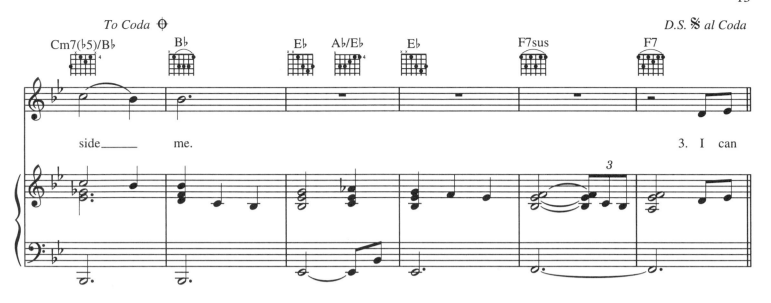

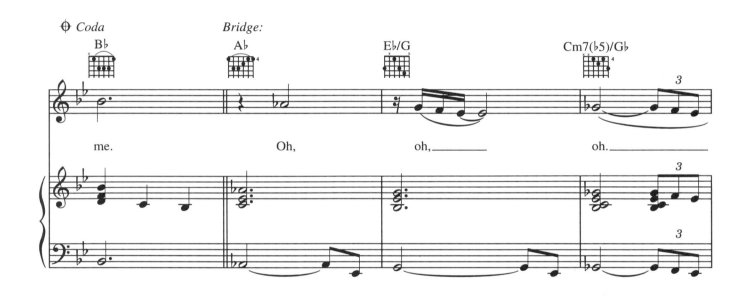

Chorus:

Misled

Words and Music by
PETER ZIZZO and JIMMY BRALOWER

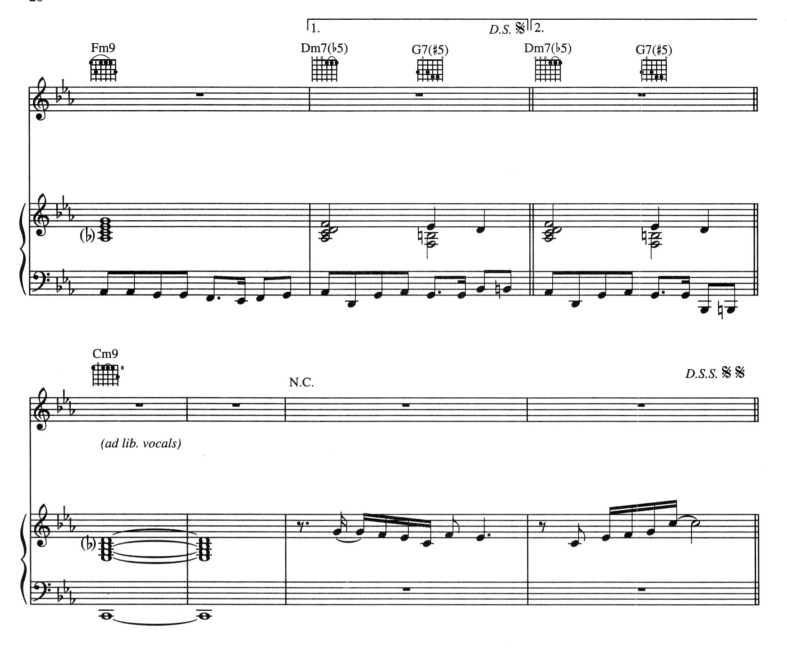

Verse 2:
Lovin' somebody ain't your average 9 to 5.
It takes conviction, it takes a will to survive.
I'm not somebody who commits the crime and leaves the scene.
But when I've been dissed, I don't spend much time on what might've been.

Bridges 2 & 3:
I'm not about self-pity, your love did me wrong,
So I'm movin', movin' on.
(To Chorus:)

The Colour Of My Love

Words and Music by
DAVID FOSTER and ARTHUR JANOV

The Power Of Love

Words by
MARY SUSAN APPLEGATE
and JENNIFER RUSH

Music by
CANDY DEROUGE
and GUNTHER MENDE

Bridge:

When I Fall In Love

Words by
EDWARD HEYMAN

Music by
VICTOR YOUNG

If You Asked Me To

Words and Music by
DIANE WARREN

Verse 2:

2. Some-how ev - er since I've been a - round you, can't go back to be - ing

on my own.___ Can't help feel - ing, dar - ling, since I've found you,___ that I've

found my___ home,___ that I'm fi - nal - ly home._____ I said I'd nev-er let no-bod-y get too

close to me,___ dar - lin'.___ I said I need-ed, need-ed to be free.___ But

D.S. % al Coda

Think Twice

Words and Music by
ANDY HILL and PETE SINFIELD

Slowly ♩ = 66

(with pedal)

Verse:

1. Don't think I can't feel that there's some-thing wrong._____
2. *See additional lyrics*

You've been the sweet-est part of__ my life_ for so____ long.   I look in your eyes   there's a

Verse 2:
Baby, think twice for the sake of our love, for the memory,
For the fire and the faith that was you and me.
Baby, I know it ain't easy when your soul cries out for higher ground,
'Cos when you're halfway up, you're always halfway down.
But baby, this is serious.
Are you thinking 'bout you or us?
(To Chorus:)

Chorus 4:
Don't do what you're about to do.
My everything depends on you,
And whatever it takes, I'll sacrifice.
Before you roll those dice,
Baby, think twice.

Where Does My Heart Beat Now

Words and Music by
TAYLOR RHODES and
ROBERT WHITE JOHNSON

Moderately slow

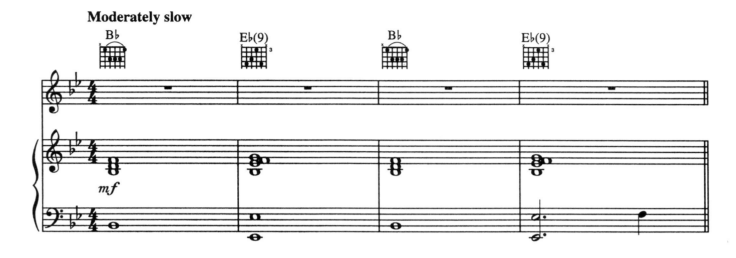

Verse:

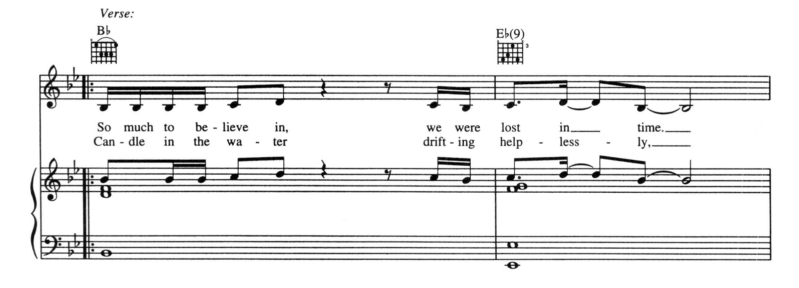

So much to be - lieve in,   we were lost in____ time.____
Can - dle in the wa - ter   drift - ing help - less - ly,____

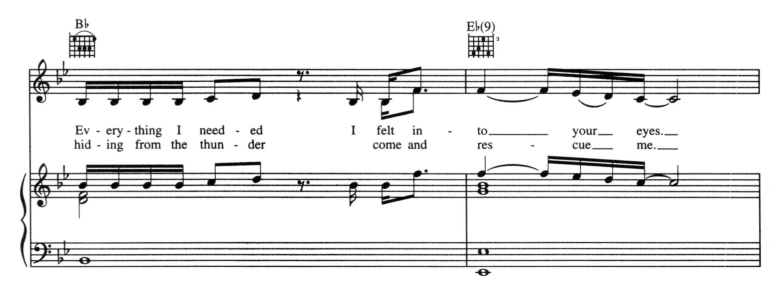

Ev - ery-thing I need - ed   I felt in - to____ your__ eyes.__
hid - ing from the thun - der   come and res - cue__ me.__

Unison

Words and Music by
BRUCE ROBERTS and ANDY GOLDMARK

1. Some-where to - night,

61

Love Can Move Mountains

Words and Music by
DIANE WARREN

Moderate rock ♩ = 100

Verse:

There ain't a dream that don't have___ a chance_ to come true___ now. It just takes___
O-ceans deep and moun - tains high,___ they can't stop___ us be-cause love___

___ a lit - tle faith,___ ba - by. An - y - thing that we want___
___ is on our side,___ ba - by. We can reach the heav - ens and touch___

Water From The Moon

Words and Music by
DIANE WARREN

Slowly ♩ = 66

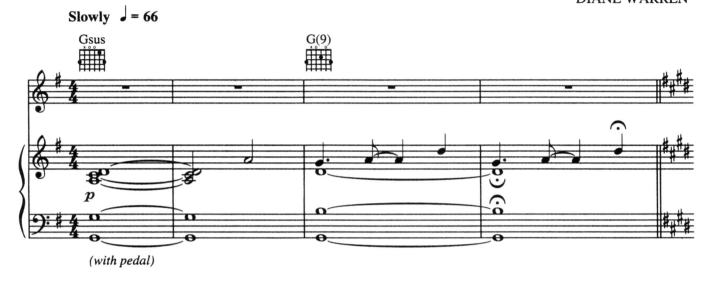

(with pedal)

Verse:

1. I've looked ev-'ry-where I can just to find___ a clue,___ oh,___ to get___

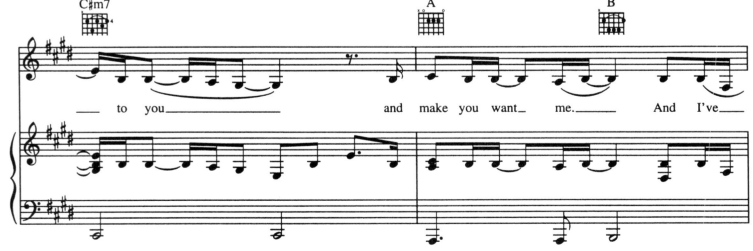

___ to you___ and make you want___ me.___ And I've___

Chorus:

What do I got-ta do?_____ Do I got-ta get

wa-ter from_ the moon?___ Is that what I got-ta do_____ to

make_ you love_ me, make_ you love_ me?_____ Do I got-ta turn the

sand in-to____ the sea?____ Is that what you want from me?_____ I've

make_ you love_ me, make_ you love_ me?_____ Do I got-ta turn the

sand in-to__ the sea?_____ Is that what you want from me?_____ I've

done ev-'ry-thing_ that I__ can do,_____ but get wa-ter from_ the moon._

Love me, how do I make you love_ me?__ How do I make you see_____ that

Celine Dion Discography

CÉLINE • INCOGNITO

INCOGNITO
LOLITA (Trop Jeune Pour Aimer)
ON TRAVERSE UN MIRROIR
PARTOUT JE TE VOIS
JOURS DE FIÈVRE
D'ABORD C'EST QUOI L'AMOUR
DÉLIVRE-MOI
COMME UN COEUR FROID

DION CHANTE PLAMONDON

DES MOTS QUI SONNENT
LE MONDE EST STONE
J'AI BESOIN D'UN CHUM
LE FILS DE SUPERMAN
JE DANSE DANS MA TÊTE
LE BLUES DU BUSINESSMAN
PIAF CHANTERAIT DU ROCK
UN GARÇON PAS COMME LES AUTRES (Ziggy)
QUELQU'UN QUE J'AIME, QUELQU'UN QUI M'AIME
LES UNS CONTRE LES AUTRES
OXYGÈNE
L'AMOUR EXISTE ENCORE

CÉLINE DION • UNISON

(If There Was) ANY OTHER WAY
IF LOVE IS OUT THE QUESTION
WHERE DOES MY HEART BEAT NOW
THE LAST TO KNOW
I'M LOVING EVERY MOMENT WITH YOU
LOVE BY ANOTHER NAME
UNISON
I FEEL TOO MUCH
IF WE COULD START OVER
HAVE A HEART

CÉLINE DION

LOVE CAN MOVE MOUNTAINS
SHOW SOME EMOTION
IF YOU ASKED ME TO
IF YOU COULD SEE ME NOW
HALFWAY TO HEAVEN
DID YOU GIVE ENOUGH LOVE
IF I WERE YOU
BEAUTY AND THE BEAST
(from the original motion picture soundtrack)
performed by Céline Dion and Peabo Bryson
I LOVE YOU, GOODBYE
LITTLE BIT OF LOVE
WATER FROM THE MOON
WITH THIS TEAR
NOTHING BROKEN BUT MY HEART

CELINE DION • THE COLOUR OF MY LOVE

THE POWER OF LOVE
MISLED
THINK TWICE
ONLY ONE ROAD
EVERYBODY'S TALKIN' MY BABY DOWN
NEXT PLANE OUT
REAL EMOTION
WHEN I FALL IN LOVE
(Featured in The TriStar Motion Picture
"Sleepless In Seattle")
Performed by Celine Dion and Clive Griffin
LOVE DOESN'T ASK WHY
REFUSE TO DANCE
I REMEMBER L.A.
NO LIVING WITHOUT LOVING YOU
LOVIN' PROOF
JUST WALK AWAY
THE COLOUR OF MY LOVE

CÉLINE DION À L'OLYMPIA

DES MOTS QUI SONNENT
WHERE DOES MY HEART BEAT NOW
L'AMOUR EXISTE ENCORE
JE DANSE DANS MA TÊTE
CALLING YOU
ELLE
MEDLEY STARMANIA
(Quand on Arrive en Ville, Les Uns Contre les Autres,
Le Monde est Stone, Naziland, ce Soir on Danse)
LE BLUES DU BUSINESSMAN
LE FILS DE SUPERMAN
LOVE CAN MOVE MOUNTAINS
ZIGGY (Un Garçon Pas Comme les Autres)
THE POWER OF LOVE
QUAND ON N'A QUE L'AMOUR

CÉLINE DION • D'EUX

POUR QUE TU M'AIMES ENCORE
LE BALLET
REGARDE-MOI
JE SAIS PAS
LA MÉMOIRE D'ABRAHAM
CHERCHE ENCORE
DESTIN
LES DERNIERS SERONT LES PREMIERS
J'IRAI OÙ TU IRAS
J'ATTENDAIS
PRIÈRE PAÍENNE
VOLE